D1416273

Life Skills

Making Tough Decisions

Working Through Hard Choices

by Robert Wandberg, PhD

Consultants:
Roberta Brack Kaufman, EdD
Dean, College of Education
Concordia University
St. Paul, Minnesota

Millie Shepich, MPH, CHES
Health Educator and District Health Coordinator
Waubonsie Valley High School
Aurora, Illinois

LifeMatters
an imprint of Capstone Press
Mankato, Minnesota

Thank you to Heather Thomson of BRAVO Middle School, Bloomington, Minnesota; to Christine Ramsay of Kennedy High School, Bloomington, Minnesota; and especially to all of their students, who developed the self-assessments and provided valuable stories and input.

LifeMatters Books are published by Capstone Press
PO Box 669 • 151 Good Counsel Drive • Mankato, Minnesota 56002
http://www.capstone-press.com

Printed in the United States of America

Library of Congress Cataloging-in-Publication Data
Wandberg, Robert.
Making tough decisions / by Robert Wandberg.
              p.   cm. — (Life skills)
        Includes bibliographical references and index.
        Summary: Explains a six-step method for making decisions and provides tips on setting goals, dreaming, and planning for the future.
        ISBN 0-7368-0697-0 (hardcover)—ISBN 0-7368-8838-1 (softcover)
        1. Decision making in adolescence—Juvenile literature. [1. Decision making.] I. Title.
        BF724.3.D47 W36 2000
        155.5′1383—dc21   00-027290
                                                                                              CIP

Staff Credits
Charles Pederson, editor; Adam Lazar, designer; Katy Kudela, photo researcher

Photo Credits
Cover: UPmagazine/©Tim Yoon
FPG/©Barbara Peacock, 30; ©Kent Miles, 49; ©Telegraph Colour Library, 54; ©Michael Krasowitz, 59
Unicorn Stock Photos/19; ©Aneal Vohra, 17; ©Jeff Greenberg, 37, 52
Uniphoto/©Gilmore J. Dufresne, 7; ©Billy E. Barnes, 9; ©Dave Schaeffer, 23; ©Daemmrich, 38;
©Llewellyn, 41; ©S. H. Begleiter, 44; ©Rick Brady, 46
UPmagazine/©Tim Yoon, 5, 15, 25, 33, 43, 51

Table of Contents

Chapter Overview

Every day, you make hundreds of decisions. Some are easy, others are more complicated.

With your independence comes the opportunity to set goals related to health, friendships, family, school, and work. Goals help tell where you are and where you want to go.

Lifestyle has the biggest effect on a person's health. Many teens need practice to say no to unhealthy lifestyle choices.

Knowing what your values are helps you to resist pressure.

Self-assessments can be a good way to learn about yourself.

CHAPTER 1

Making Decisions

Making Decisions

Most of us make hundreds of decisions every day. Many of the day-to-day decisions we make do not have major positive or negative consequences. We decide when to get up in the morning and what to eat. We decide what clothes to wear or what route to take to school or the bus stop. Decisions such as these are usually easy and don't require much effort. However, this book will look at more difficult decisions related to setting goals and planning for the future. You will also understand that **DecisionMatters** can help you make tough decisions to reach your goals.

Susie rolled over sleepily and looked at her alarm clock. "Oh, no! It's after seven! I must not have heard the alarm ring." The reality of the day flooded over her. She thought about what was going on that day: school pictures, math quiz, a football game.

She could hear her dad's footsteps coming toward her door. "Your sister beat you to the shower. There probably won't be any hot water left. Oh yeah, Will called. He can't pick you up this morning." Susie wondered if she even wanted to get out of bed.

Within minutes of waking up, Susie faced many decisions:

It's picture day. She wants to look her best. What will she wear? How will she get her hair washed? The shower will be cold.

Should she skip school, since she's already late? If she does, she can't go to the football game.

If she doesn't go to school, when will she make up the math quiz? If she takes the quiz today, when will she study?

How will she get to school because Will can't drive her there?

There won't be time to eat anything before class. Should she just wait until lunch?

Making Tough Decisions

Decisions may have positive or negative consequences. For example, if Susie does decide to study, her positive consequence may be a good grade. If she doesn't study, the negative consequence may be a bad grade. Susie's decisions require some thought, but they probably won't change her life. However, some decisions that people make are difficult and may have serious consequences.

Many of a person's most difficult decisions involve health and well-being. Few of a person's life goals can be accomplished without health. For example, if a person has a heart disease, he or she probably can't run in a marathon. Health-related decisions you make today can limit future education, career, or family ambitions. For example, choosing to use certain drugs may seriously affect your ability to conceive children.

What Are Goals?

Teens are learning to become adults. They might be testing their independence for the first time. They are beginning to think about who they are and what they want in life. This means they must set goals about what they want to accomplish. There are two kinds of goals: short-term and long-term goals. Chapter 4 describes them more closely. Setting goals is a way to see where you want to go and how to get there.

FAST FACT

The American Medical Association reports that the leading lifestyle causes of death in the United States are (1) tobacco use, (2) poor diet and lack of exercise, and (3) alcohol use.

For example, many teens have to decide about using alcohol, tobacco, or other drugs. They often have to decide about their sexual activity. One reason that these decisions can be difficult is because they involve friendships and peer acceptance. Peer pressure to use drugs or become sexually active can be real and extremely strong. No one wants to lose friends or not be accepted. For example, the desire to be accepted may be so strong that a teen may use drugs to fit into a group.

Lifestyle Choices and Health

Some factors that affect your health and well-being include family traits, environment, and health care. The most important factor is your lifestyle, or how you choose to live. Teens with healthy lifestyles can confidently say yes to health-enhancing behaviors. These can lead to a healthy life.

Teens with a healthy lifestyle also can confidently say no to health-endangering behaviors. Any of the following six lifestyle areas require intelligent choices. Poor choices in these high-risk areas could be dangerous to a teen's health.

Tobacco use

Alcohol and other drug use

Sexual behaviors resulting in HIV infection, other sexually transmitted diseases (STDs) or sexually transmitted infections (STIs), or unintended pregnancy

Eating patterns that contribute to disease or illness, such as eating lots of high-fat or high-calorie foods

Lack of physical activity

Behaviors that result in intentional or unintentional injury to yourself or other people, such as murder or a car accident

Everyone makes good and bad choices. Making mistakes is one way we learn. However, people who decide carefully generally can make good choices. They can get their needs met and accomplish goals.

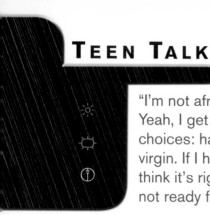

TEEN TALK

"I'm not afraid to admit I've decided to stay a virgin for now. Yeah, I get teased, and that can hurt. But I only see two real choices: have sex because everyone thinks I should, or stay a virgin. If I have sex, I'll feel terrible afterward because I don't think it's right. Having sex with someone is a big step, and I'm not ready for those feelings yet."—Paco, age 17

What Are Values?

To make good decisions, it helps to know what your values are. Values are the principles, standards, or qualities that you think are good or desirable. Sometimes you feel pressure to behave in ways that oppose your parents' values, others' values, or your religious values. By knowing your values, you can resist such pressures better.

Usually, teens can choose to say yes or no. Sometimes saying no is difficult because of strong peer pressure. Many teens need practice to say no effectively to unhealthy lifestyle choices. Later chapters in this book will help you practice making healthy decisions.

We never outgrow the need to make good decisions. Can you make tough decisions about your personal health? Do you make responsible decisions that may affect the health of your family, friends, and community? Chapter 2 offers a method for making good choices related to health.

Self-Assessments

Self-assessments are tests that help us recognize our connection to an issue. They can give information that helps predict your success, attitudes, or health risks. Self-assessments usually include questions about knowledge, attitude, and behavior relating to a topic or situation. Periodically assessing yourself can help you keep track of what is normal for you. The key to self-assessments is that you are the one who interprets the information. Teens developed the self-assessment on page 12. It can help you see how well you make decisions about your health. It contains items that many teens believe are important.

How Healthy Am I?

Read items 1–15 below. Following each item, circle the number that best describes you. Use this rating scale as you circle the numbers.

Never = 1   Sometimes = 2   Always = 3

Item	Never	Sometimes	Always
1. I exercise for at least 30 minutes, 3 times a week.	1	2	3
2. I avoid trying to lift more than I think I can carry.	1	2	3
3. I warm up and stretch before exercising.	1	2	3
4. I eat healthy, well-balanced meals.	1	2	3
5. I limit my snacks.	1	2	3
6. I avoid eating a lot right before sleeping.	1	2	3
7. I get at least 7 to 8 hours of sleep every night.	1	2	3
8. I avoid tobacco.	1	2	3
9. I avoid alcohol.	1	2	3
10. I avoid illegal drugs.	1	2	3
11. I avoid risky sexual behaviors.	1	2	3
12. I feel physically fit.	1	2	3
13. I have a positive view of life.	1	2	3
14. I wear a seat belt.	1	2	3
15. I avoid riding with a driver who has been drinking or using other drugs.	1	2	3

Add up your points. The closer your total is to 45, the better you are at making health-enhancing decisions. Feel good about the items you scored 3 on. You probably need some practice on items where you scored a 1 or 2.

"Those who stand for nothing fall for anything."
—Alexander Hamilton, first secretary of the U.S. Treasury

Points to Consider: DecisionMatters

What do you think are the most difficult decisions that teens regularly have to make?

Which of the 6 health factors on page 9 do you think present the highest risk for teens?

How do you think goals and values are different from each other?

Give an example of how your values might support a health goal.

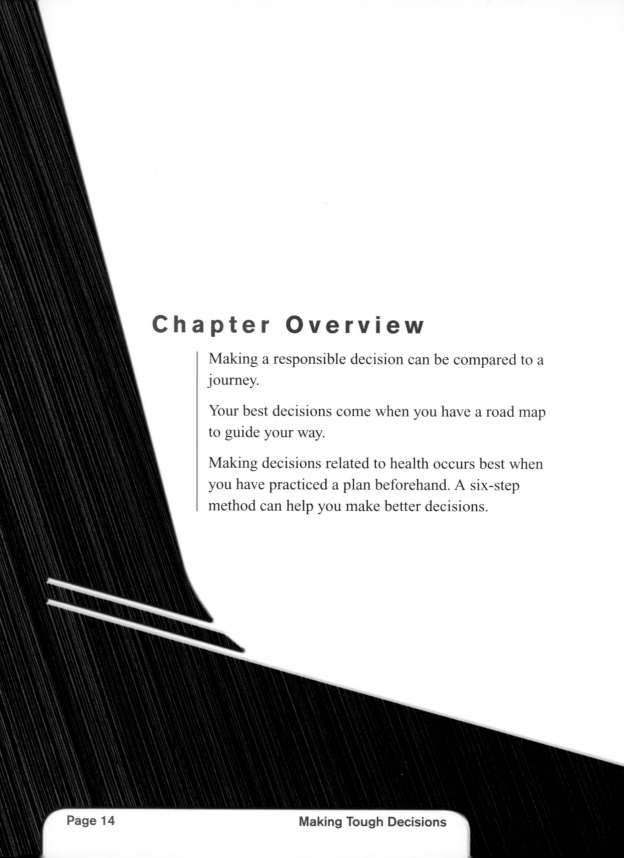

Chapter Overview

Making a responsible decision can be compared to a journey.

Your best decisions come when you have a road map to guide your way.

Making decisions related to health occurs best when you have practiced a plan beforehand. A six-step method can help you make better decisions.

CHAPTER 2

Making a Plan

To make a decision, it is often helpful to have a plan. In this chapter, you will learn a six-step decision-making method. A key part of this method is to determine how much time you have to decide. Knowing the urgency of a decision might be called **TimeMatters.**

MYTH VS. FACT

Myth: Once you make a decision, you can't change your mind. Other people will think less of you if you do change it.

Fact: You can always change your mind. Sometimes the situation changes or you learn more information. Then changing your mind might be the smartest thing to do.

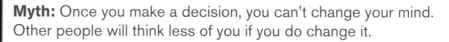

Molly and Marq, Ages 19 and 18

Molly had pulled the car over to the roadside. Molly asked Marq, "We're lost, aren't we? Didn't you bring the map?"

Marq looked embarrassed. "No," he finally mumbled.

Molly asked, "What do you mean? I asked you before we left if you had it. You said you did. Now how are we supposed to find our way?"

The Journey to a Decision

Road maps are designed to guide travelers on their trip. If you were traveling to an unfamiliar location, you might want to use a map to avoid getting lost. Similarly, when you need to make decisions, you need a kind of map. Such a guide to make a tough decision may keep you from getting lost.

On a road map, you may have to take several routes to reach your final destination. Likewise, to reach an important decision, you may need several steps to reach your final choice.

Making Tough Decisions

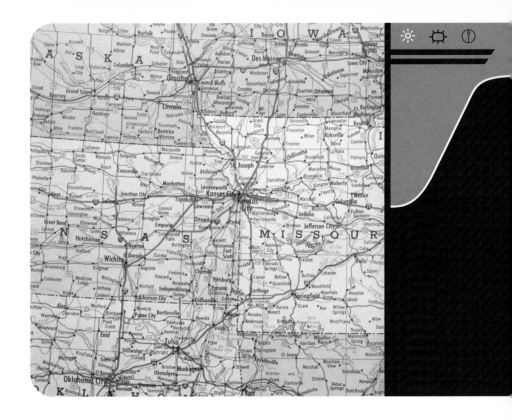

A Decision-Making Road Map

Making a decision might seem confusing at times. However, there are ways to make it easier. For example, the following is a six-step method for making tough, responsible decisions. Think of these six steps as a handy road map to find your way. This method works well for small decisions. It works equally well for big, important decisions.

1. Identify the decision. You need to clearly understand the decision you are making. It often helps to state it out loud or write it down. For example, you might say, "I need to decide if I should exercise more." Don't combine several decisions. For example, don't decide whether to lose weight and whether to be sexually active at once. Look at each decision separately.

2. Decide how important a decision is. The next step is to determine how important a decision is. You can do this by knowing the priority of the decision. The priority tells you the order in which you need to act on decisions. The amount of time that's available for the decision can tell you the priority. Some decisions are about low-priority problems, crisis decisions, or emergencies.

A low-priority problem has low risk or danger. You often don't have to decide right away about a low-priority problem. For example, you may want to decide what classes to take next semester. You might take several days or even weeks. It's often enough to consider and plan for these problems for now. You have to decide on high-priority problems right away, even if they don't affect your health. An example of this kind of problem might be what clothes to wear to a party tonight.

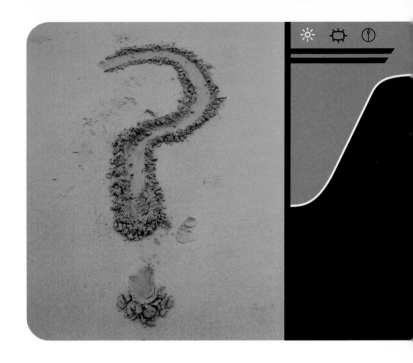

A crisis is more serious than a problem. The final decision you make has real potential for high risk or danger. Some crises are low priority. You may be able to wait on the decision for a while. For example, you may be deciding whether to have sexual intercourse. You might have time to decide, but your decision could deeply affect you now and in the future. If the crisis is high priority, you must decide right away what to do.

An emergency requires your immediate decision so you can take action. Like a crisis, an emergency is risky or dangerous. For example, imagine someone threatens you with violence, or your friend considers killing himself. You must decide on the spot how to react. By not acting at once, you may be risking your life or someone else's.

3. Identify choices. Decisions usually involve more than one choice. You must determine what those choices are. Often a parent, friend, or trusted, responsible adult can help you think of several choices. These people may even identify some choices that you hadn't considered. If it's not a crisis, brainstorm choices. That is, think of all the choices you can without judging any of them. Even think of silly or impossible choices. They may lead to a choice that could work. Writing down your choices can be helpful.

"I was going to drop out of school to work full time at my job. I finally decided to stay in school. I figured I might still be at the same job. So I probably could make more money after I graduated."–Tom, age 18

4. Judge the choices. After you have listed choices, judge each one carefully if you have enough time. Consider your personal values and those of your family. Values have a major influence on your decisions. Your values and ethics will help you know what's good and bad or responsible and irresponsible. Ethics are your beliefs about right and wrong.

For example, a friend might want you to skip school to see a great movie that's leaving town soon. This will be the last chance you'll get to see it. However, you might not feel comfortable skipping. You might feel that it's the wrong thing to do. Your ethics will help you decide what to do.

Look at your list of possible choices. What are the positive and negative consequences of each choice? Which choices have the greater benefits? How does each choice fit with your values and ethics? How do you think you will feel about each choice tomorrow or in a few days or weeks?

5. Select a choice. At this point, decide the best thing to do. Have confidence in your decision. Once you decide, create a plan to carry out your decision. Then put your plan into action.

6. Judge the result. After you act on your choice, review and judge what happened. Was your choice a good one? Did it need to be changed or adjusted? If your choice didn't work or needs to be changed, and if the problem or decision still exists, go back to Step 3.

Brian, Age 15

Brian was thinking about getting his tongue pierced. His friend Matty was pushing hard for him to do it. It wouldn't be the first time Brian had been pierced. His left ear already had an earring and a stud. Also, lots of Brian's friends had pierced body parts. Still, sticking something through his tongue was different. He wasn't quite sure what to do.

Do you think having a decision-making method is like having a road map? Why or why not?

What are examples of situations when teens may have to make emergency or crisis decisions?

Think of a time when you had to make a quick decision. Then think of a time you had a chance to think carefully about a decision. Which decision turned out best? Why?

Use the six steps to help Brian decide about getting his tongue pierced.

Chapter Overview

Knowledge and skill are not the same thing. It's possible to know how to do something yet be unable to do it.

People need practice in making decisions that promote health and safety.

Practice helps a person feel confident. The skill being practiced starts to occur more naturally.

CHAPTER 3

Decision Making: Knowledge vs. Skill

If you asked a softball player how to catch a ground ball, one answer might be: "Keep your eyes on the ball, bend your legs, and touch your glove to the ground." This answer shows that the softball player has the knowledge to catch a ground ball. However, does the player have the skill to catch it? Maybe yes, maybe no.

Most of us know people who have lots of knowledge about how to do something. However, they may lack the skill to do it. Is that bad? Of course not. Look at many coaches of high school, university, or professional sports teams. They might not be able to perform skills as well as their players do. However, they have the knowledge to help others perform the skill. In this chapter you will learn about **SkillMatters** in decision making. You also will practice the decision-making method you learned in Chapter 2.

The Value of Practice

Have you heard the saying "Practice makes perfect"? There are three ways people can increase their skill: practice, practice, and practice. It's essential. Rarely are athletes, musicians, or others successful without lots of practice.

The same is true of behavior. Do you know anyone who has tried to quit smoking? It is a complicated process. The person may know the risks of cigarette smoking. She or he may know the short-term problems like shortness of breath or stained fingers. Long-term difficulties can result in heart disease or other illnesses. That person may know all the reasons and may even want to quit. Without practice, the person is not likely to succeed.

Look at another example. Most teens know that they should exercise several times a week. Exercise improves a person's physical and mental health. However, many teens don't exercise. Why? They may not have enough practice at doing it.

Just knowing how to quit smoking or start exercising doesn't mean that people can do so. Making good, thoughtful decisions is a skill. To become good at it, people need to practice. With enough practice, a skill becomes habit. The person no longer has to think about it.

"We can try to avoid making choices by doing nothing, but even that is a decision."
—Gary Collins, author

Practicing the Decision-Making Method

Do you remember the decision-making method you learned in Chapter 2? Step 2 of the method is to decide how important the decision is. You must decide if the problem is high or low priority, a crisis, or an emergency.

It's important, so let's practice this second step. In your opinion, is each of these situations a problem, crisis, or emergency?

1. Judy exercises too much.

2. Carmen has been withdrawing from friendships.

3. Pedro skips breakfast.

4. Jeanne drinks large amounts of alcohol.

5. James falls asleep in class.

6. Mark is choking on some candy.

7. Chris's parents physically abuse him.

8. Clarisa has said she intends to kill herself.

9. Kari thinks she may be pregnant.

10. Stephon's mother emotionally abuses him.

It's not always easy to decide how important a decision is. Without specific details, you could view each situation in different ways. However, if you believe someone is in immediate danger, you must decide at once. Otherwise, you may need more information. This requires you to ask questions and use critical thinking skills.

Heather, Age 15

Heather and some friends are going to a movie Friday night. After the movie they plan to meet at another kid's home for a party. Heather knows that some of the kids who will be there smoke marijuana. She is worried that they will ask her to try some. She knows it could be dangerous, and that scares her a little. She tried cigarettes once, which made her feel sick. Heather wonders if she'd feel the same way with marijuana. She also knows that her parents would kill her if they caught her using pot. However, she's worried what the other kids will think of her if she doesn't try it.

Making Tough Decisions

Heather isn't sure how to deal with this situation. The six-step method from Chapter 2 can help Heather figure out her situation.

1. Identify the decision. First Heather needs to decide whether to go to the party after the movie. If she goes, then she will need to decide what to do about using marijuana.

2. Decide how important a decision is. Deciding about the party may be a low-priority problem. She has some time to make a decision. However, deciding about pot may be a crisis because her decision could affect her future. Neither decision is an emergency because Heather doesn't have to make an immediate life-or-death decision.

3. Identify choices. Heather can attend or avoid the party. If she attends, she must decide whether to smoke pot. If she avoids the party, she could find something else to do with friends or by herself.

4. Judge the choices. If Heather avoids the party, her friends might give her a hard time. However, she may miss a fun time. If she attends and is offered pot, she could agree or refuse. If she agrees, she will probably fit in better with the other kids. However, she might feel sick or her parents might find out. She worries about doing something really stupid if she tries pot. If she chooses to refuse the marijuana, she needs to decide how to do that.

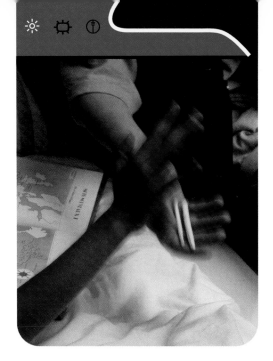

5. Select a choice. Let's say that Heather chooses to attend the party. She also decides she doesn't want to use pot. She talks with her friend May, who also doesn't use it. Heather asks if she and May can hang out together at the party. They might feel stronger to know someone else won't be using.

Heather thinks that some of the people at the party might keep pressuring her to use. She and May decide to help each other practice saying no in a firm but friendly way. For example, she tries, "No thanks. I don't like it." She thinks about people's reaction to that and comes up with a few other responses. She and May agree to leave together if people don't respect their decision.

6. Judge the result. After the party, Heather asks herself questions about how she felt about her decisions. Did she have fun? Did she feel comfortable saying no? Did people respect her decision? Did her decisions fit her values? How might her decisions affect her long-term goals? Would she make the same decision in the future?

Points to Consider: SkillMatters

What is the difference between health knowledge and health skill?

Describe a time when you practiced a skill. Did you get better? Did the skill become a habit?

How do you think this saying is related to decision making: "An ounce of prevention is worth a pound of cure"?

Do you think Heather made reasonable decisions? Could she have done anything differently? How?

Chapter Overview

Maslow's hierarchy describes how people fulfill their needs. It can be helpful in setting goals.

Maslow believed people have five needs: physical, safety, belonging, self-esteem, and self-actualization.

Achieving a goal may take time.

Everyone has needs. Goals are how people try to meet those needs.

Goals are usually short term or long term.

CHAPTER 4

Setting Goals

What will you be doing next week, next year, or in 10 years? This is a difficult question for some teens. Do your answers involve people, places, school, career, family, or children? Setting goals for your near or distant future can be helpful as you face today's tough decisions. In this chapter you will learn about setting these **GoalMatters**.

Maslow's Hierarchy

Abraham Maslow was an American psychologist. He developed what is called Maslow's hierarchy. A hierarchy shows the order or importance of something. Maslow's hierarchy shows the importance of people's needs. Maslow believed that five needs motivate people in this order: (1) physical, (2) safety, (3) belonging, (4) self-esteem needs, and (5) self-actualization. This hierarchy is much like climbing a ladder or going up steps. To get to the next higher step, you have to stand on the one below it.

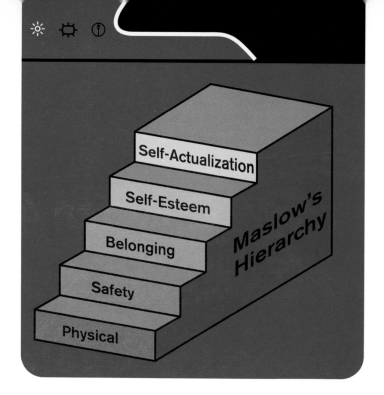

Maslow believed that it's possible to achieve the highest level of health. For that to happen, all five levels of needs must be satisfied in a positive way. By using positive life skills to climb Maslow's hierarchy, a person is more likely to be healthy.

Sometimes people try to meet their needs in negative, damaging ways. For example, to meet the need for safety, people might join a gang. Gang members may feel safer among a group of people who agree to protect each other. However, it is likely that gang members won't be safer. They may become targets of rival gangs. They might be arrested and put in prison. Instead of being safer, gang members often end up less safe. Using a negative way to meet a personal need for safety could be a health risk.

Physical Needs

The most basic of all human needs are physical. For example, water, food, and sleep are necessary for survival. If these needs are not met, a person will die.

Safety Needs

The need for safety is the second level in Maslow's hierarchy. People want to live in a safe place and be free of worry. Protection from crime or having appropriate clothing are examples of safety needs. Most people in North America can fulfill their physical and safety needs.

Belonging Needs

The third level of Maslow's hierarchy is the need to belong. Most people need to fit in with a social group and have relationships with other people. Those who meet this need can love and be loved and have friends.

Tina and Beverly, Age 17

Tina and Beverly were new in school. They both wanted to make friends and fit in with a group. Tina was interested in acting, so she joined the theater club. She made many friends. Beverly didn't have many interests or hobbies. She found a group that liked to drink alcohol. They accepted her without question, and she made many friends.

"A musician must make music, an artist must paint, and a poet must write."—Abraham Maslow

Self-Esteem Needs

The need for self-esteem is the fourth level of Maslow's hierarchy. Self-esteem is a belief in the value of self and others. One way people can satisfy this need is to feel good about and respect themselves and others. Self-confident people often believe they can succeed at tasks. These people can say no to unhealthy choices or pressures. People with strong self-esteem also can say yes to healthy lifestyle choices.

Jarrell and Vincent, Age 14

Jarrell was walking home from the bus stop. At the door to his apartment building, another boy stopped him. He asked if Jarrell wanted to make some money selling drugs. Jarrell said, "No thanks," and kept walking. Vincent approached the door a couple of minutes later. The same boy stopped him. Vincent thought he probably should walk past but didn't want to seem rude. Anyway, it seemed like it might be pretty easy money.

Self-Actualization

The highest level of Maslow's hierarchy is self-actualization. This means that a person fulfills his or her creative urges. Your interests and passions motivate you and drive you toward this level. Maslow called this drive a person's calling, or what the person is born to do.

A calling may not be the same as a job or career. For example, Renata is taking classes to become an auto mechanic. In her spare time, she plays in a band. She likes her mechanical studies, but music makes her feel alive. Joe works part time in a day care center. However, he spends every spare moment either in his garden or learning about gardening. Don't think of self-actualization as a reward for fulfilling a need. Think of it as a need in itself.

Needs and Goals: What's the Difference?

How can we tell the difference between needs and goals? Needs are
something all people have, even if they are not aware of it. Goals are the
way each individual seeks to meet the need. People will likely have different
goals to meet the same need. For example, two people may be meeting the
need for self-esteem. One may choose to become a professional athlete. The
other may study hard to pass the next math quiz. Each person has a different
goal, yet each goal builds that person's self-esteem.

Along the way to reaching a goal, people make decisions. If their goal
changes, people usually make different decisions. For example, to meet
physical needs, a person might have the goal of getting a job to buy food.
If the person can't get a job, she or he might steal food. The physical need
of having to eat hasn't changed. However, the goal has changed in meeting
the need.

Look at the following situations. Which of Maslow's five levels of needs do you believe is the main motivator? The answers in parentheses are suggestions only. Some situations might fit in more than one level. Some people don't choose health-enhancing ways to meet a need.

1. Barbara assists with serving food at a homeless shelter. (self-actualization)

2. George smokes marijuana. (physical)

3. Susan goes to the movies with her friends. (belonging)

4. Bill joins the football team. (self-esteem)

5. Ling decides to go to college. (belonging)

6. Franco injects illegal body-building drugs called steroids. (self-esteem)

7. Mindy steals a bag of apples. (physical)

8. Tim buys a gun. (safety)

9. Hanna gets to school early to eat breakfast with her friends. (belonging)

10. Erika travels to Europe. (self-actualization)

Short-Term and Long-Term Goals

Do you have difficulty making decisions? Do you want to make your decision-making process easier? Try setting goals. If you have clear and consistent goals, many of your decisions will be easier. Our goals give us purpose and direction. Goals can usually be either short term or long term.

Short-term goals usually can be achieved in a short period of time. Some short-term goals might be eating more fruits and vegetables, working longer on homework, or exercising more. Long-term goals usually are more difficult and take longer to achieve. Some examples are getting better grades in school or entering a particular career. Other examples include maintaining appropriate body weight or avoiding tobacco.

Megan, Age 19

Megan lived in North Dakota. It was January and Megan was talking with her friend Eileen. "I want to go to California this summer," she said.

"Why?" asked Eileen.

Megan replied, "I've never been there, and it seems like there's lots to do. Also, my stepdad has family he hasn't seen for a long time, and it'd be nice to surprise him."

"When would you plan to go?" asked Eileen.

Megan answered, "My goal would be to get out there no later than August."

Does Megan have a short-term goal or a long-term goal? It might be considered a long-term goal. She'll need time to plan and make the arrangements. However, with a firm goal, she will have an easier time focusing on what needs to be done.

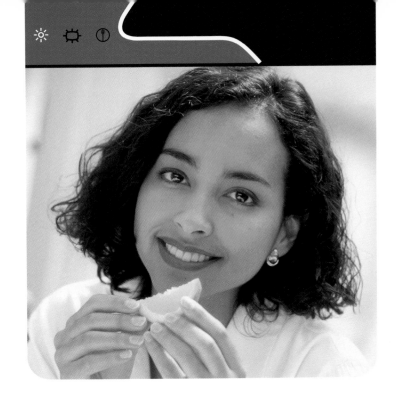

To achieve many long-term goals, short-term goals need to be achieved first. One of Megan's short-term goals might include getting in touch with her stepfather's family. Another goal might be to figure out what any tours or sight-seeing will cost.

What are some important short-term goals in your life? What are the important long-term goals? Take time to think about them seriously.

Points to Consider: GoalMatters

How do you think human needs and motivations are related?

Do you think Maslow's hierarchy accurately describes human behavior? Why or why not?

Have you ever had a long-term goal? How did you try to achieve it? What short-term goals did you have to reach along the way?

Chapter Overview

To set appropriate goals, you need to understand yourself. A decision may be easier if you can relate it to a goal that you have set for yourself.

Achieving goals depends on decision making.

Making good decisions and setting goals can help you reach your dreams. Some suggestions for setting goals include choosing goals that fit you, sharing them with others, and being persistent.

You are in charge of your goals. This helps you be in control of your future.

Making Tough Decisions

CHAPTER 5

Making Dreams Happen

A dream is the best future you can imagine. When you dream of the future, do you think of money, romance, adventure, or success? Many of your dreams can come true. For most people, dreams don't come true by just wishing. Their achievement depends on preparing for and making some tough decisions about the future. These **DreamMatters** are worth the effort. In this chapter you will learn how decision making and goal setting can help you reach your dreams.

Future Goals and Present Decisions

One of the first steps in setting goals is to think about who you are. Socrates, a philosopher of ancient Greece, said: "Know thyself." Knowing yourself will help guide you in reaching your goals.

How do you get to know yourself? One way is to identify your values and needs. Your values may change. For example, you might think money is important now. Later, you may think friendships, having children, or getting a job you love are more important than money.

Your needs tell you a lot about yourself. For example, some people need to be around other people. They spend all the time they can with friends. Other people need time alone. They might feel nervous in large groups. Be careful when seeking to satisfy a need. The emotional and physical well-being of you and others are important to consider.

Sometimes satisfying your needs may affect the needs of someone else. For example, John likes to keep to himself. He doesn't like to talk about his personal life with everyone. Eric, however, loves to tell everyone, even strangers, what's happening in his life. He also expects them to talk freely about themselves. John sometimes feels that Eric asks rude questions that make him feel uncomfortable.

Making Tough Decisions

"My teacher asked me what plans I had after I graduated. I said I didn't have any plans and I didn't care that much. Then he said, 'It doesn't matter which way you go then, does it?' I guess he meant that it's easier figuring out what to do if you have a goal."–Adam, age 18

Developing a Clear Direction

Why do we need goals? Why can't life just happen? Without goals, dreams, or destinations, many people never feel a sense of purpose in their life. Knowing yourself and what's important to you will help you identify your dreams for the future. When your dreams are in place, you have the foundation for making decisions to achieve them.

Your decision making pretty much determines whether you reach your goals and dreams. Teens who learn how to make good decisions are likely to reach their dreams. They are also likely to become healthy, caring, and responsible adults.

Thinking about yourself and your goals is a lifelong process. As your goals change, you also change your decisions about reaching your goals.

Goal-Setting Ideas

Here are some suggestions for setting and reaching the goals that will guide your tough decision making.

Select goals that are yours, not someone else's. You are the best person to set goals for yourself. You know yourself best and what you want and need. Other people probably have goals for you, too. In most cases, their goals for you are well-intended. However, what they want may not be what you want. For example, your school counselor might think you should get a particular job. That's okay if you have the same goal. If you don't, tell the person what your goal is. Then stick to it.

Share your goals with others. Telling your goals to other people is often a good idea. They may be able to support you on your journey. People who care about you won't ask you to do things that will keep you from reaching your goals. Finding someone who will support you could even be a short-term goal.

Get the information and skills to keep you on track. Preparing for success is critical. You may have seen runners prepare for a race by stretching. In the same way, you should prepare to reach your goals. Get the facts, details, education, and skills to accomplish your goals. For example, find out what classes you need to get into a college. Find out how much practice you need to become a pro athlete. If you work hard, you will be hard to beat!

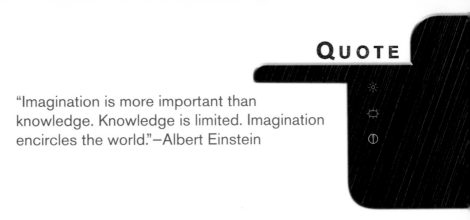

"Imagination is more important than knowledge. Knowledge is limited. Imagination encircles the world."—Albert Einstein

Be flexible. Everyone makes mistakes. The mistakes that you make help direct you toward your goals. We all talk to ourselves. Sometimes we are negative and say, "Give up." Sometimes we are positive and say "Keep going" and "You did it." The challenge is to give ourselves only positive messages. That way, if situations change, the positive voices will help us change, too, rather than give up.

Shoot for the stars. Dreams can be as wild and wonderful as your creativity and imagination can make them. Your goals should be big enough to encourage, excite, and inspire you. They also should be realistic enough that you believe you can reach them. For example, maybe you wanted to be a sports star but have come to believe that's impossible. Don't shut the door on related possibilities. Your goal instead could be to become a professional sports announcer or a coach, for example.

Be persistent. Don't give up or get discouraged when something doesn't happen just the way you want. Accept that there will be setbacks. It may be helpful to adjust your plans to overcome obstacles. Keep trying. Using the decision-making method from Chapter 2 will be helpful.

Have fun. Enjoy the adventure of pursuing your goals. Sometimes the journey can be as satisfying as the destination.

FAST FACT

The Search Institute in Minneapolis conducted a survey of teens. According to the survey, 70 percent of youth have a positive view of their future.

You Have the Power!

Who controls your goals? Sometimes it may seem that teens have little control over what happens to them. However, power and control are a matter mostly of attitude. People who feel in control of their own goals often believe they control what happens. People who feel they have no control believe that things just happen to them. They feel no power to change anything. You are the one who can and should be in control.

Lisa, Age 17

Lisa had worked in the same job for a year. It was time for her job review, but her boss hadn't mentioned it. Lisa began to worry she had done something wrong, though she couldn't imagine what. Her friend Lou finally told her, "Maybe nothing's wrong. But if there is, it's best to find out. Ask your boss about it. Don't just wait for her. You can't improve if you don't know what the problem is. Anything's better than imagining the worst." Lisa agreed.

Later, she told Lou, "My boss said she had been so busy she forgot my review. Not only was nothing wrong, but she said I was doing great work. Then she gave me a raise! I'm so relieved."

Points to Consider: DreamMatters

What does "Know thyself" mean to you? List ways you might use to know yourself.

List two long-term goals you have. Who could support you in reaching them?

Do you agree or disagree that mistakes help people learn? Explain.

How might adults help you in setting and reaching goals?

Do you feel in control of your goals? If not, how could you help yourself feel more in control?

Chapter Overview

Goals are usually built on many small decisions.

Good health habits build on each other. Doing one thing in a healthy way often makes it easier to have other good health habits.

Writing a behavior contract can help you reach a goal of health.

CHAPTER 6

Planning for Achievement

Committing Yourself to Good Health Habits

Good planning is the foundation to reach your goals and dreams. It's possible that a single poor decision could devastate you. For example, choosing to drink and drive could lead to an accident that changes your life. Luckily, reaching your goals is usually built on many smaller decisions. For big goals, your decisions may be spread over several years.

Many of the decisions you make relate to your health. Planning for good health will take you a long way toward achieving your goals and dreams. These **PlanMatters** are important to you later in your life.

Dolores, Age 17

"I used to smoke, and so did most of my friends. Finally, I decided to quit. I tried a bunch of different ways before I found one that worked. It was hard, but I'm glad I quit. Quitting smoking has made it easier for me to reach other goals. I eat better these days. I feel like exercising now. I didn't at all while I was smoking. After I quit smoking, I also felt better about saying no to other risky stuff, like unprotected sex."

Like adults, teens usually have both healthy and unhealthy habits. Choosing good health habits often leads to other good decisions about health. For example, people who exercise tend to eat better than people who don't exercise. On the other hand, one poor health habit can lead to other poor health habits. For example, people who overeat may avoid the doctor. They may be afraid the doctor will say their health is poor because of their eating.

Writing a Behavior Contract

One way to start the process of developing and maintaining good health habits is to write a behavior contract. This is a written promise to yourself that you will plan to have a healthier lifestyle. Good decision making is necessary at all steps of writing the contract. You'll need paper and pencil, then follow these steps.

1. Consider. We all have some areas of health that could use some improvement. Think about all the possibilities to improve your life. You probably won't write down anything at this step. Here are some areas to think about improving:

Body weight

Alcohol and other drug use

Tobacco use

Physical activity

Sexual behavior

Car safety

Study habits

Family or peer relationships

Rest and sleep needs

Stress

2. Pick. Choose an area from Step 1 that you want to improve. Pick something that you believe you can succeed at. Write it down.

3. Write. Write a description of your present behavior in the health area you've chosen.

4. Look ahead. Write down where you want to be in a few weeks in your area. When writing this section, use terms that you can measure and that involve numbers. For example, state how often you want to do something. You might write "exercise 5 times a week" or "meditate twice a day for 30 minutes."

5. Make a plan. Write your weekly plan to achieve your goal. Specifically, what are you going to do? What decisions will be necessary? For example, "I will not go to parties where alcohol is served." Or "I will not get in a car with a driver who has been drinking."

6. Plan your goal. Write the health improvements you hope to see at the end of the time you set.

7. List obstacles. Write at least two obstacles you expect as you plan for your goal. In other words, what might prevent you from reaching your goal? What will be the most difficult decisions you have to make?

8. List supporters. At the bottom of the page, leave space for the date, your signature, and another person's signature. This might be a friend or relative who will witness and support this contract. Ask your witness to check on your progress at least once a week. The witness can call you, talk in person, e-mail, or check with you in other ways. This person's support can be helpful if you struggle to complete your contract.

"My neighbor down the hall always used to say, 'If you fail to plan, you plan to fail.' I never understood that until he showed me one way to plan. You write down the positives and negatives of a situation. Then you decide if the negatives or positives are more important to you. Sometimes when you can see them written out, it's easier to decide what to do. That was pretty good advice."—Leo, age 19

9. Track. On the back of your paper, draw a chart to keep track of your weekly progress for the next few weeks.

10. Summarize. Write a summary at the end of the contract period. Did you achieve your goal? Why or why not? How do you feel about your accomplishment? Which decisions were easy? Which were hard? Why?

If you stick with it, you will likely succeed. When you do, know that you have succeeded because you chose to. If you don't succeed, accept that, too, and try again. The sample contract on page 58 shows how Steps 2 through 8 might be written.

Michelle's Contract to Get More Sleep

Step	What the contract might say
2. Pick.	I'm going to choose the "rest and sleep needs" area from Step 1.
3. Write.	Right now, I get to bed between 11:00 and 12:00 every night. Usually I'm up late because I have to do homework. I have to get up at 6:00 A.M. to catch the bus. I feel pretty sleepy by midmorning.
4. Look ahead.	At the end of five weeks, I want to be getting at least eight hours of sleep every school night.
5. Make a plan.	I'm going to quit watching so much TV earlier in the evening. I have to find a time when I can do my homework instead. From 8:00 to 10:00, I'll do homework for at least an hour. Then I'll go to bed at 10:00. If I finish my homework early, I'll read or play a game with my brother.
6. Plan your goal.	The extra sleep should help me feel more alert during school. I also hope it makes getting up easier. Right now I feel pretty crabby at 6:00 in the morning.
7. List obstacles.	I don't want to miss my favorite show from 7:00 to 8:00. But afterward, I usually just sit and flip the channels. I do that for at least an hour hoping something good will be on. The hardest part of reaching my goal will be turning off the TV after my show.
8. List supporters.	Date _____ My Name _____ Witness's Name _____

How do you think choosing one healthy behavior might make it easier to choose another?

Why might writing a contract be helpful to change a poor health behavior?

Choose one of the areas in Step 1 on page 54. Write a behavior contract to improve your health in that area. What do you think might happen?

NOTE

At publication, all resources listed here were accurate and appropriate to the topics covered in this book. Addresses and phone numbers may change. When visiting Internet sites and links, use good judgment.

Internet Sites

American Cancer Society
1-800-ACS-2345 (1-800-227-2345)
www.cancer.org/tobacco/index.html
Topics related to smoking

Canadian Health Network
www.canadian-health-network.ca/customtools/homee.html
Links to health topics in Canada

Go Ask Alice!
www.goaskalice.columbia.edu/index.html
Factual, straightforward answers to teens' questions about emotional, sexual, physical, and spiritual health

Iwannaknow.org
www.iwannaknow.org
Information on teen sexual health

Teenwire
www.teenwire.com
Information on sex, life, and other teen issues

Useful Addresses

American Social Health Association
PO Box 13827
Research Triangle Park, NC 27709
www.ashastd.org

Centers for Disease Control and Prevention
(CDC)
1600 Clifton Road
Atlanta, GA 30333
www.cdc.gov/tobacco

National Institute on Alcohol Abuse and
Alcoholism (NIAAA)
6000 Executive Boulevard
Willco Building
Bethesda, MD 20892-7003
www.niaaa.nih.gov

Planned Parenthood
810 Seventh Avenue
New York, NY 10019
www.plannedparenthood.org

For Further Reading

Benson, Peter L., Judy Galbraith, and Pamela Espeland. *What Teens Need to Succeed: Proven, Practical Ways to Shape Your Own Future.* Minneapolis: Free Spirit, 1998.

Bunnell, Jean. *You Decide! Making Responsible Choices.* Grand Rapids, MI: Instructional Fair, 1998.

Covey, Sean. *The Seven Habits of Highly Effective Teens.* New York: Simon and Schuster, 1998.

Gray, Heather M., and Samantha Phillips. *Real Girl/Real World: Tools for Finding Your True Self.* Seal Press, 1998.

Glossary

crisis decision (KRYE-suhss di-SIZH-uhn)—an action taken after several hours or days to reduce potential risk or danger

emergency decision (uh-MUR-juhn-see di-SIZH-uhn)—an action that requires an immediate response because of high risk or danger

ethics (ETH-iks)—beliefs about right and wrong that guide a person's behavior

health-endangering behavior (helth-en-DAYN-jur-ing bi-HAYV-yur)—high-risk behavior that may involve sexual activity, drug use, or eating practices

health-enhancing behavior (helth-en-HANSS-ing bi-HAYV-yur)—behavior that promotes values, beliefs, and goals leading to a healthy life

hierarchy (HYE-ur-ar-kee)—the order or importance of a group of things

lifestyle (LIFE-stile)—the way a person chooses to live

priority (prye-OR-uh-tee)—the order of importance; high-priority decisions should be made before low-priority decisions.

self-actualization (self-ak-choo-wuhl-uh-ZAY-shuhn)—the fulfillment or accomplishment of a person's creativity

self-esteem (self-ess-TEEM)—a person's belief in the value of herself or himself and others

sexually transmitted disease (STD) (SEK-shoo-wuhl-lee tranz-MIT-uhd duh-ZEEZ)—herpes, gonorrhea, syphilis, or other diseases spread by sexual contact; STDs also are called sexually transmitted infections (STIs).

value (VAL-yoo)—a principle, standard, or quality that a person considers good or desirable